The system consists of 6 Steps most horses can be ignored at Step 1.

Important

Firstly we are only interested in UK Handicap Races Class 4, 5 and Class 6.

→ **Please exclude National Hunt Flat (Bumper) races and Hunter Chases.**

Below outlines the system and is then followed by example races in detail over the flat and jumps racing for 2019.

Choose a UK flat or jump races were the class of the race is 4,5,6 (not Bumpers or Hunter chases).

I have found that Class 4 and (Class 6 especially AWF all weather flat races) have a great strike rate.

It is important you do not rush the races and ensure the horses meet the correct criteria. This is where many punters fail, they do not do the homework!

You are only looking to get one bet right and collect your profit.

Once you have selected a race look at each horse in the race and apply the following process to each horse in turn. You will soon become familiar with the process and will be able to qualify horses very quickly in your chosen race.

We will use the following horse as an example **"Fontley House"** that ran at Kempton 3-10 on the 25th November 2019.

Below is the screenshot from the Racing Post.

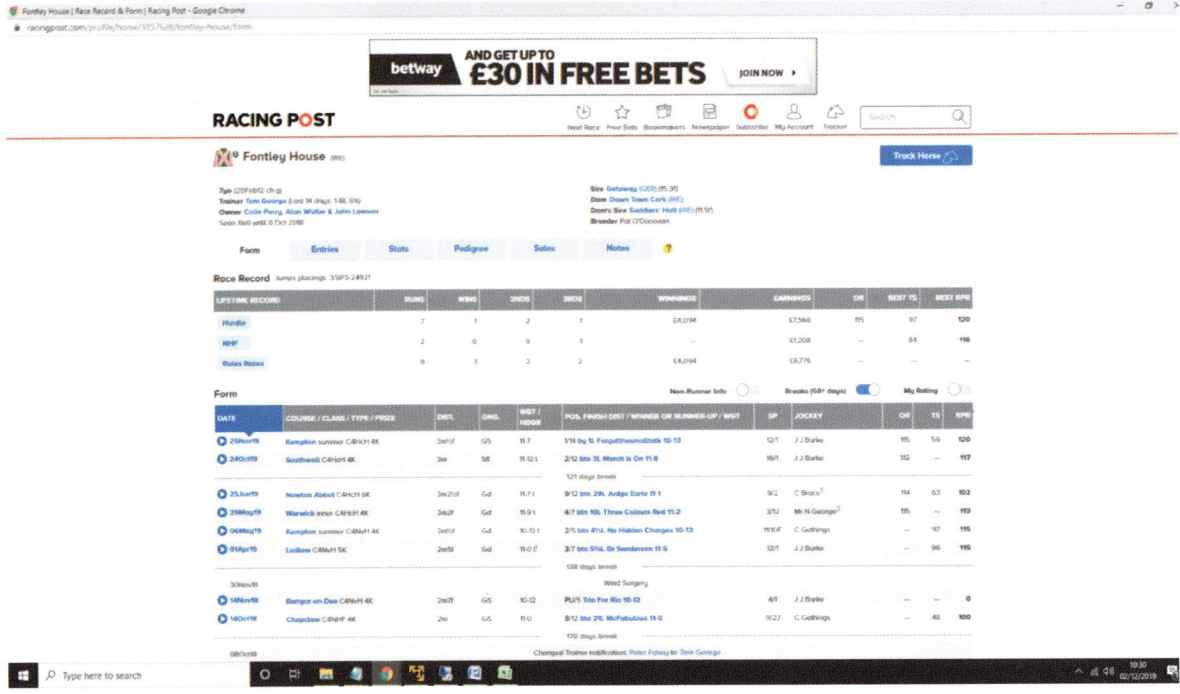

Step 1). The horse selected must not have run more than 12 times in it's lifetime in any type of race novice, maidens, handicap races. Only move to the next step if the horse satisfies this criteria.

You can see **"Fontley House"** had run 9 times this is next to the column **Rules Races 9** but it was actually 8 as it includes the race on the 25th November 2019 which obviously you would not see on the day's racing as we are looking at the past here.

So in order to check how many times a horse has run in it's lifetime use the value in the column **'Rules Race'**

This step will eliminate many horses in the race you have decided to look at for a possible selection for a bet.

You must only move to the next step with the horse you are processing if it passes this step!

If not move on to the next horse in the race and repeat this step (1).

Step 2). For the horse identify it's last **handicap** race where it finished in the top 5 positions i.e. 1,2,3,4,5

You will see that **"Fontley House"** last handicap race was on the 24th October 2019 where it finished 2nd in a Class 4 HcH – Handicap Hurdle at Southwell.

So this horse qualifies for the next step.

You must only move to the next step with the horse you are processing if it passes this step!

Step 3). In the horse's last handicap race **24th October 2019** selected in step 2 above you need to record the horse's BHB (OR – Official Rating) and weight it raced off.

You will see the BHB OR column next to the **Jockey** column

SP	Jockey	OR	TS	RPR
16/1	J J Burke	112	-	117

So the last BHB or OR is 112

Please take a note of this.

We also need to take note of the weight it raced off which is under the column **WGT/HDGR**

DIST.	GNG.	WGT / HDGR
3m	Sft	11-12

So **"Fontley House"** last raced off a weight 11 stone 12 pounds 11-12

There are 14 pounds to a stone!

Now we know the last handicap race the horse ran and it's BHB or OR and the weight it raced off. We also know it finished in the top 5 positions in a handicap race.

Now move on to the next step!

Step 4). Note down the horse's current BHB (OR – Official Racing) and it's weight i.e. what it is running in today's race.

You can get this information from the Race Card in the Racing Post under the column

Horse	Age	WGT OR
Fontley House	7	**11-7**

An example race card

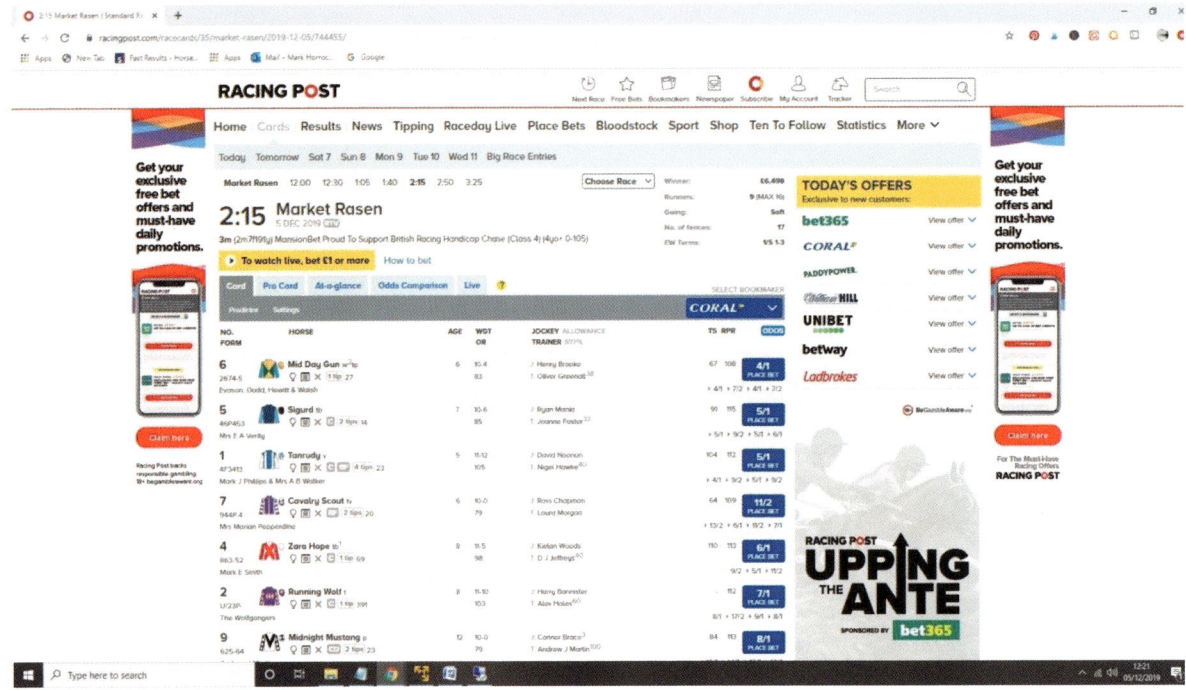

Step 5). Subtract the BHB OR value noted down in Step (3) above from the BHB OR value noted down in Step (4)

So the calculation is as follows,

115-112=3

Step 6). Subtract the weight value in Step (3) above from the weight value in Step (4)

-→ The weight must be expressed in pounds not stones and pounds

So the calculation is as follows,

There are 14 pounds in a stone

It's last race weight **11-12** which is 11 stone 12 pounds is 11*14 = 154 pounds

154 + 12 =166

Today's race weight,

11-7 which is 11 stone and 7 pounds is 11*14 = 154 pounds

154 + 7 =161

So 161-166=-5 pounds (Minus 5 pounds).

Summary

You need to repeat Steps 1 to 6 for each horse in the selected race and note down the following values,

Horse	BHB Diff	Weight Diff
Fontley House	3	-5

For a horse to qualify as a bet the value of BHB Diff must be greater than or equal to 0 and the value of Weight Diff must be less than or equal to 0

Note you might have more than one selection for a race!

I ignore races with more than 2 selections.

I go into this race in more detail in A. Example Races.

How To Process Races Quickly

1. Choose UK handicap races only Class 4,5,6 **(not Bumpers or Hunter chases).**
2. For a given handicap race only pick horses who have had less than or equal to 12 total runs. This should eliminate many horses in the race you are analysing and save time.
3. For each horse selected in (2) above identify the last handicap race the horse finished in the last 5 positions i.e. 1st, 2nd, 3rd 4th or 5th
4. If the horse qualifies in (3) then note down the horse's BHB (OR – Official Rating) and weight carried by the horse in that qualifying handicap race then perform the following subtractions:

BHB_DIFF = Horse's current race BHB rating - Horse's last Handicap race BHB rating

WEIGHT_DIFF== Horse's current race weight (pounds) - Horse's last handicap race weight (pounds)

5. Are there any selections in the race?

You should have the following list for a race,

Horse	BHB_DIFF	WEIGHT_DIFF	Does The Horse Qualify As A Bet
Fontley House	3	-5	YES

Example Races

The following Race examples show more information that is needed but I wanted you to see the full picture. We are only interested in the RED and YELLOW highlighted values.

The columns to concentrate on are the BHB Diff and WEIGHT DIFF!

Qualifying horses to place a bet on are highlighted in **BOLD**

Race 1

25th November 2019   Kempton 3.10 Fontley House   Winner : 12/1

Class 4

Fontley House highlighted in bold is the only horse that satisfies the criteria and is a great bet at 12/1 and even bigger on Betfair!

Horse	Result Date	Current BHB	Last BHB	BHB DIFF	WEIGHT DIFF	Last POSITION	Last WIN Date	Total Runs
Bold Record	2019-17-08	119	120	-1	6	3	100	5
Muthabir	2019-20-02	115	118	-3	9	5	278	31
Forgetthesmalltalk	2017-23-12	114	118	-4	-11	2	702	7
Ramore Will	10/04/2019	116	116	0	10	2	52	26
Pontresina	2019-15-10	116	115	1	8	2	41	7
Fontley House	**2019-24-10**	**115**	**112**	**3**	**-5**	**2**	**32**	**8**
Cracker Jak	2019-22-10	108	109	-1	4	4	34	12
Sandy Boy	11/05/2019	115	108	7	3	4	20	11
Espalion	2019-26-04	117	107	10	1	1	213	10
Max Forte	2019-22-05	115	106	9	-6	3	187	25
Id Better Go Now	2019-27-10	109	102	7	2	1	29	5
Vlannon	05/02/2019	118	51	67	40	2	207	6
Montys Angel	2019-25-10	108	49	59	40	3	31	14
Saturdaynightfever	2018-19-11	110	0	110	4	3	371	8

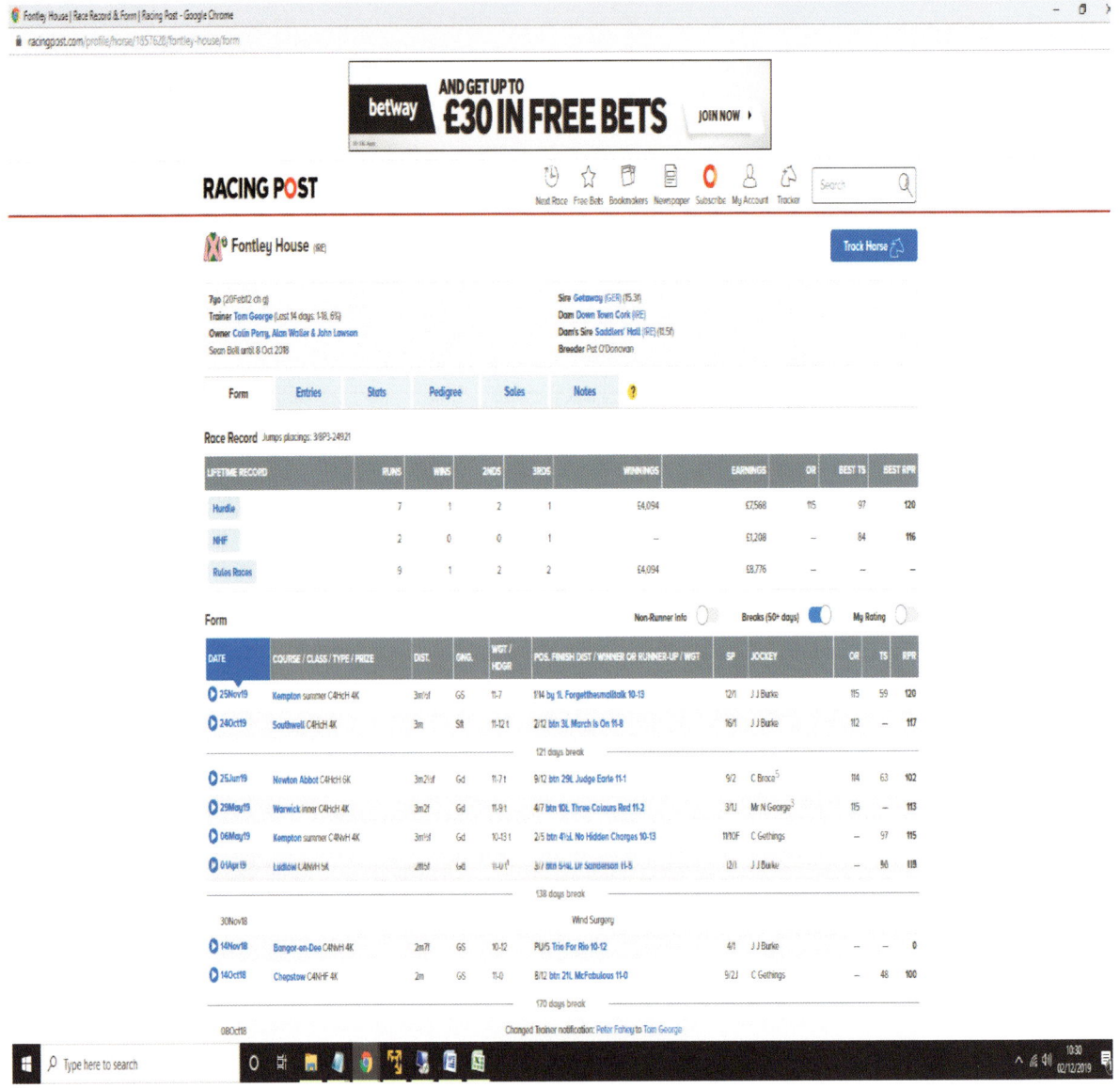

The screenshot show total runs as 9 as it includes the race on the 25/11/2019. But at the time of the race the horse had only run 8 times.

You can see from the screenshot the horse Fontley House last run was on the 24th October 2019 where the horse finished 2nd. The horse was carrying weight of 11-12 i.e. 11 stone 12 pounds and had a BHB or Official rating (OR) of 112.

When Fontley House ran in the race 25th November, 2019 it was carrying weight of 11-7 i.e. 11 stone 7 pounds so the horse was carrying less -5 pounds in weight!

The horse Fontley House BHB (OR) rating was 112 when it ran on the 24th October, 2019 as compared to the BHB (OR) to 115 when it ran on the 25th November 2019. So the horse had improved by 3.

Summary

This was a very good bet indeed and at a nice price! The horse was improving from it's last run from a BHB (OR – Official rating) of 112 to 115 and was down 5 pounds in the weights.

The horse won the race at a SP of 12/1 but on Betfair the horse traded in-play at 17.0.

Race 2

25th November 2019   Mussleburgh 1.55 Im Too Generous Winner : 10/1

Class 4

Horse	Result Date	Current BHB	Last BHB	BHB DIFF	WEIGHT DIFF	Last POSITION	Last WIN Date	Total Runs
Trongate	2019-13-04	107	123	-16	16	5	226	27
Keep The River	2019-15-01	108	114	-6	4	3	314	11
Trapper Peak	2019-18-10	116	109	7	17	1	38	50
Nefyn Bay	2019-24-10	107	107	0	9	4	32	40
Something Brewing	08/02/2019	107	106	1	11	1	115	16
Im Too Generous	**2019-15-05**	**107**	**102**	**5**	**-1**	**3**	**194**	**10**
Lastofthecosmics	11/06/2019	95	96	-1	7	3	19	8
Potters Away	10/06/2019	90	92	-2	-20	5	50	7
Iconic Belle	2019-29-06	110	76	34	33	3	149	8
Beast Of Belstane	11/03/2019	110	0	110	14	5	22	7
Buttevant Lady	11/07/2019	110	0	110	14	2	18	3

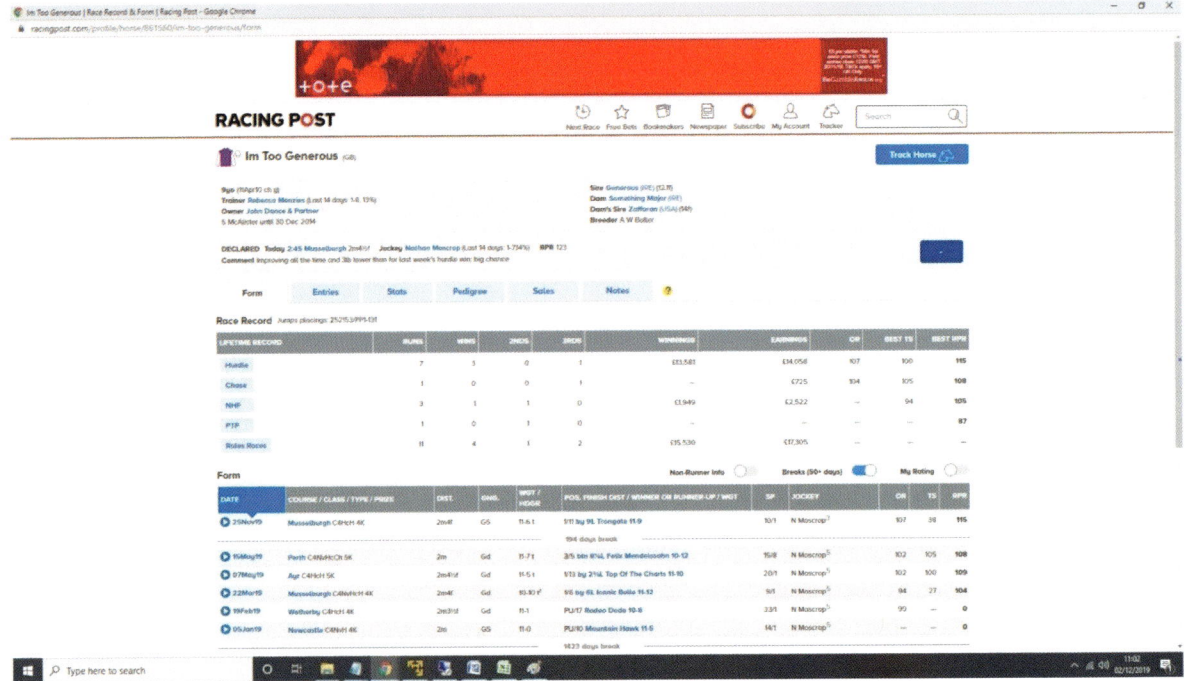

The screenshot show total runs as 11 as it includes the race on the 25/11/2019. But at the time of the race the horse had only run 10 times.

You can see from the screenshot the horse IM Too Generous last run was on the 15th May 2019 where the horse finished 3rd. The horse was carrying weight of 11-7 i.e. 11 stone 7 pounds and had a BHB or Official rating (OR) of 102.

When IM Too Generous ran in the race 25th November 2019 it was carrying weight of 11-6 i.e. 11 stone 6 pounds so the horse was carrying less -1 pounds in weight!

The horse Im Too Generous BHB (OR) rating was 102 when it ran on the 15th May, 2019 as compared to the BHB (OR) to 107 when it ran on the 25th November 2019. So the horse had improved by 5.

Summary

A good bet and a nice price. The horse was improving from it's last run from a BHB (OR – Official rating) of 102 to 107 and was down 1 pounds in the weights.

The horse won the race at a SP of 10/1 but on Betfair the horse traded in-play at 12.5.

Race 3

25th November 2019   Ludlow 3.50 Urtheonethatiwant Winner : 7/2

Class 4

Horse	Result Date	Current BHB	Last BHB	BHB DIFF	WEIGHT DIFF	Last POSITION	Last WIN Date	Total Runs
His Dream	2019-15-10	106	109	-3	13	4	41	23
Our Delboy	2017-25-04	90	106	-16	-14	4	944	9
Artichoke Heart	2019-24-10	101	97	4	5	2	32	10
Love The Leader	11/08/2019	100	97	3	-1	2	17	44
Urtheonethatiwant	**04/09/2019**	**94**	**90**	**4**	**0**	1	230	**10**
Agent Westy	10/05/2019	87	85	2	-6	1	51	11
Isla Di Milano	2019-19-06	78	80	-2	-3	4	159	8
The Lion Man	2018-23-05	72	74	-2	5	1	551	30

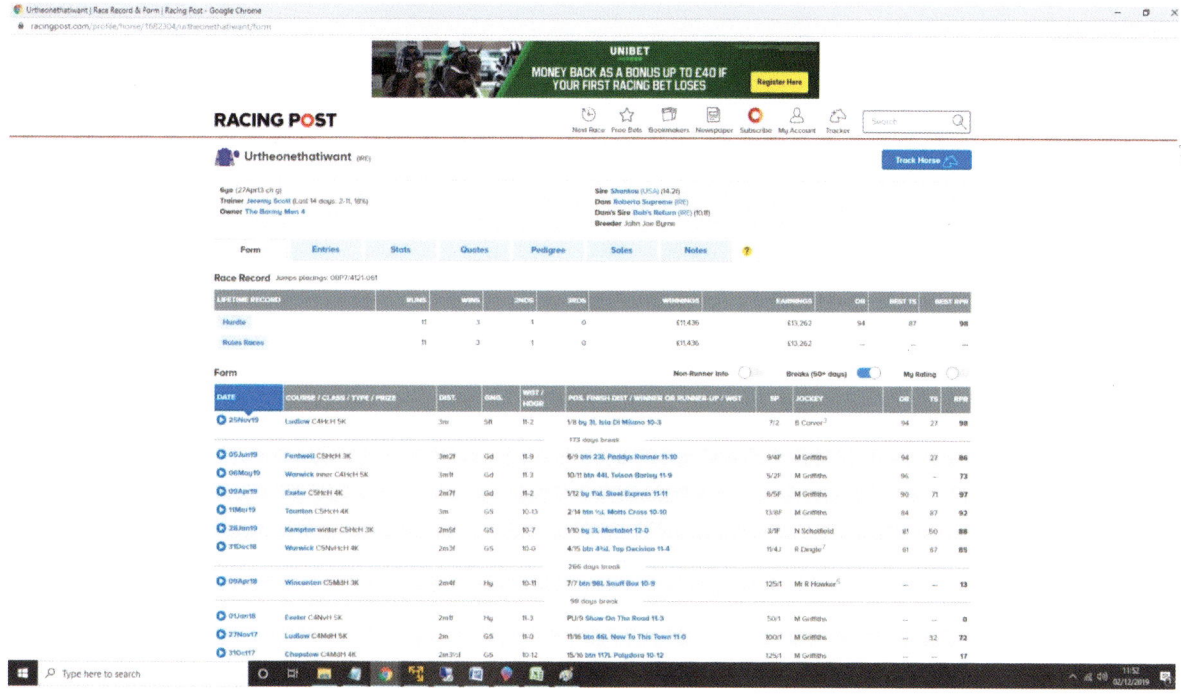

The screenshot above shows total runs as 11 as it includes the race on the 25/11/2019. But at the time of the race the horse had only run 10 times.

You can see from the screenshot the horse Urtheonethatiwant last run was on the 9th April 2019 where the horse finished 1st. The horse was carrying weight of 11-2 i.e. 11 stone 2 pounds and had a BHB or Official rating (OR) of 90.

When Urtheonethatiwant ran in the race 25th November, 2019 it was carrying weight of 11-2 i.e. 11 stone 2 pounds so the horse was carrying the ==same weight== as in it's last qualifying race.

The horse Urtheonethatiwant BHB (OR) rating was **90** when it ran on the 09th April, 2019 as compared to the BHB (OR) to **94** when it ran on the 25th November 2019. So the horse had improved by ==4==.

Summary

Not a good price as I like double figured priced horses. The horse was improving from it's last run from a BHB (OR – Official rating) of 90 to 94 and was carrying the same weight as in it's last race back in April.

The horse won the race at a SP of 7/2 but on Betfair the horse traded in-play at 8.6.

Race 4

28th November 2019   Taunton 2.15   Don Lami   Winner : 16/1

Class 4

Horse	Result Date	Current BHB	Last BHB	BHB DIFF	WEIGHT DIFF	Last POSITION	Last WIN Date	Total Runs
Forgot To Ask	2019-26-06	122	123	-1	19	3	155	15
Montys Award	2019-28-09	122	122	0	9	3	61	14
Dentley De Mee	2019-23-10	120	122	-2	12	4	36	20
Monkey Puzzle	2019-23-09	119	120	-1	7	2	66	6
Don Lami	**2018-27-05**	**120**	**118**	**2**	**0**	**2**	**550**	**6**
Innisfree Lad	2018-28-03	106	115	-9	-12	3	610	12
Manofthemountain	10/01/2019	120	114	6	0	1	58	5
Benechenko	2018-16-05	110	114	-4	-7	4	561	11
Lex Talionis	2019-20-04	108	111	-3	-3	4	222	23
Battle Of Ideas	2019-17-11	109	109	0	-3	2	11	18
Apple Mack	11/04/2019	107	105	2	0	2	24	8
Halloween Harry	12/05/2018	109	0	109	-1	3	358	5
Putdecashonthedash	04/12/2019	100	0	100	-6	3	230	4

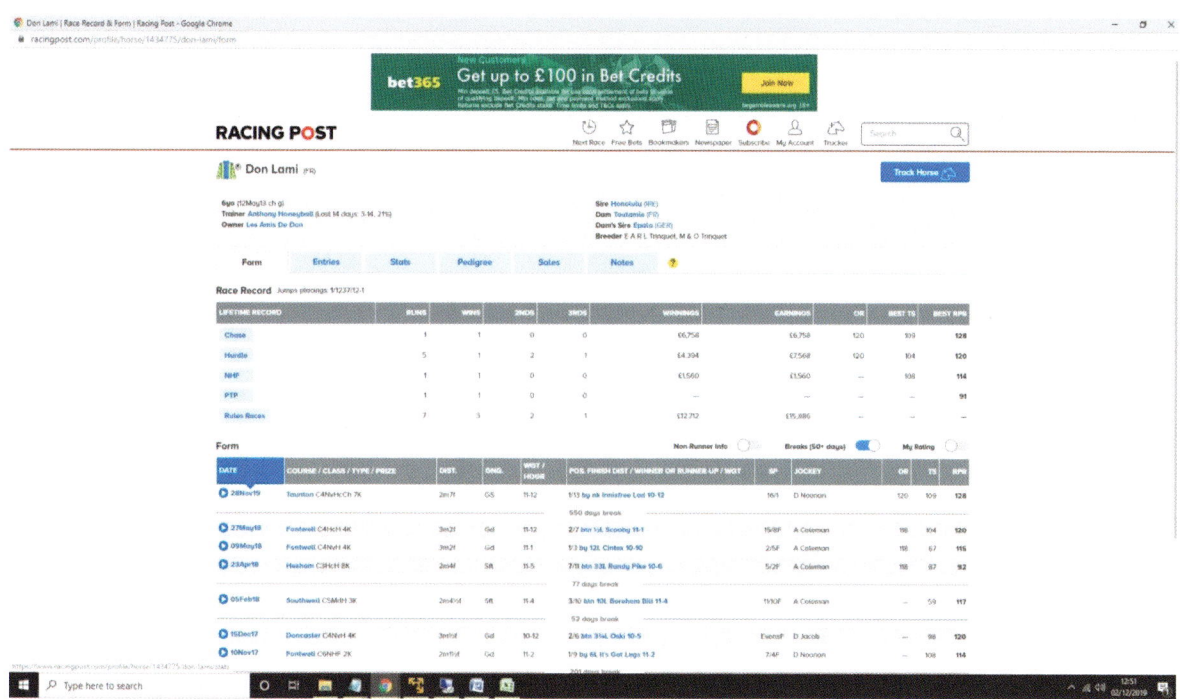

The screenshot above shows total runs as 7 as it includes the race on the 28/11/2019. But at the time of the race the horse had only run 6 times.

You can see from the screenshot the horse Don Lami last run was on the 27th May 2019 where the horse finished 2nd. The horse was carrying weight of 11-12 i.e. 11 stone 12 pounds and had a BHB or Official rating (OR) of 118.

When Don Lami ran in the race 28th November, 2019 it was carrying weight of 11-12 i.e. 11 stone 12 pounds so the horse was carrying the ==same weight== as in it's last qualifying race.

The horse Don Lami BHB (OR) rating was ==118== when it ran on the 27th May, 2019 as compared to the BHB (OR) to ==120== when it ran on the 28th November 2019. So the horse had improved by ==2==.

Summary

This was a great price. The horse was improving from it's last run from a BHB (OR – Official rating) of 118 to 120 and was carrying the same weight as in it's last race back in May 2019.

The horse won the race at a SP of 16/1 but on Betfair the horse traded in-play at 48.0!!!!!

Race 5

28th November 2019   Taunton 1.45 Cushuish Winner : 17/2

Class 4

Horse	Result Date	Current BHB	Last BHB	BHB DIFF	WEIGHT DIFF	Last POSITION	Last WIN Date	Total Runs
Vamanos	11/09/2019	115	115	0	14	2	19	6
Deputy Jones	11/04/2019	112	115	-3	4	5	24	4
Three Bullet Gate	2019-30-03	106	106	0	3	4	243	8
Primal Focus	2019-22-10	111	105	6	8	1	37	18
Mister Murchan	11/08/2019	98	98	0	6	4	20	5
Cushuish	2019-30-10	==96==	==94==	==2==	==-17==	2	29	==12==
Gang Warfare	04/03/2019	103	81	22	28	3	239	7
Ekayburg	2019-27-06	102	60	42	23	2	154	6
Easyrun De Vassy	12/08/2018	109	0	109	14	5	355	3
Caspers Court	02/04/2019	106	0	106	-1	3	297	4
Theatre Mix	05/08/2019	102	0	102	1	5	204	6

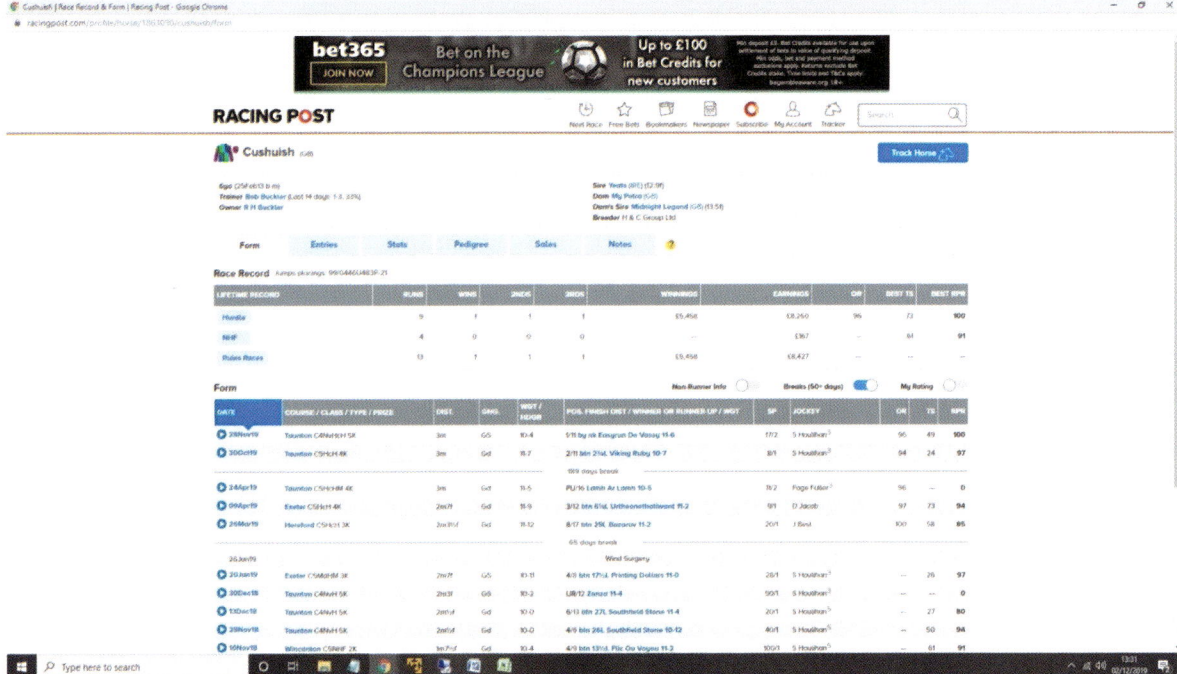

The screenshot above shows total runs as 13 as it includes the race on the 28/11/2019. But at the time of the race the horse had only run 12 times.

You can see from the screenshot the horse Cushuish last run was on the 30th October 2019 where the horse finished 2nd. The horse was carrying weight of 11-7 i.e. 11 stone 7 pounds and had a BHB or Official rating (OR) of 94.

When Cushuish ran in the race 28th November, 2019 it was carrying weight of 10-4 i.e. 10 stone 4 pounds so the horse was carrying -17 pounds less weight as in it's last qualifying race.

The horse Cushuish BHB (OR) rating was 94 when it ran on the 30th October, 2019 as compared to the BHB (OR) to 96 when it ran on the 28th November 2019. So the horse had improved by 2.

Summary

This was a great price. The horse was improving from it's last run from a BHB (OR – Official rating) of 94 to 96 and was carrying -17 pounds less weight as in it's last race back in October 2019.

The horse won the race at a SP of 17/2 but on Betfair the horse traded in-play at 55.0!!!!!

Race 6

29th November 2019   Kempton 7.00 Lord Howard Winner : 9/1

Class 6

Horse	Result Date	Current BHB	Last BHB	BHB DIFF	WEIGHT DIFF	Last POSITION	Last WIN Date	Total Runs
Toybox	09/02/2019	60	64	-4	4	3	88	14
Bolt N Brown	11/05/2019	60	62	-2	1	4	24	13
Barbarosa	2019-18-11	58	58	0	3	2	11	15
Just Once	2019-15-09	58	58	0	3	3	75	10
Barbarosa	2019-18-11	58	58	0	3	2	11	15
Just Once	2019-15-09	58	58	0	3	3	75	10
Savoy Brown	2019-27-07	45	57	-12	-7	5	125	12
Royal Dancer	2019-18-11	53	53	0	0	3	11	17
Jailbreak	06/11/2019	45	50	-5	-4	4	171	10
Lord Howard	10/08/2019	**51**	**46**	**5**	**-7**	1	52	**6**
Miss Pollyanna	09/11/2019	50	45	5	0	5	79	8
Brinkleys Katie	11/06/2019	45	45	0	6	2	23	11
Social City	11/09/2019	59	0	59	1	2	20	3
Gibraltarian	08/05/2019	54	0	54	4	5	116	4

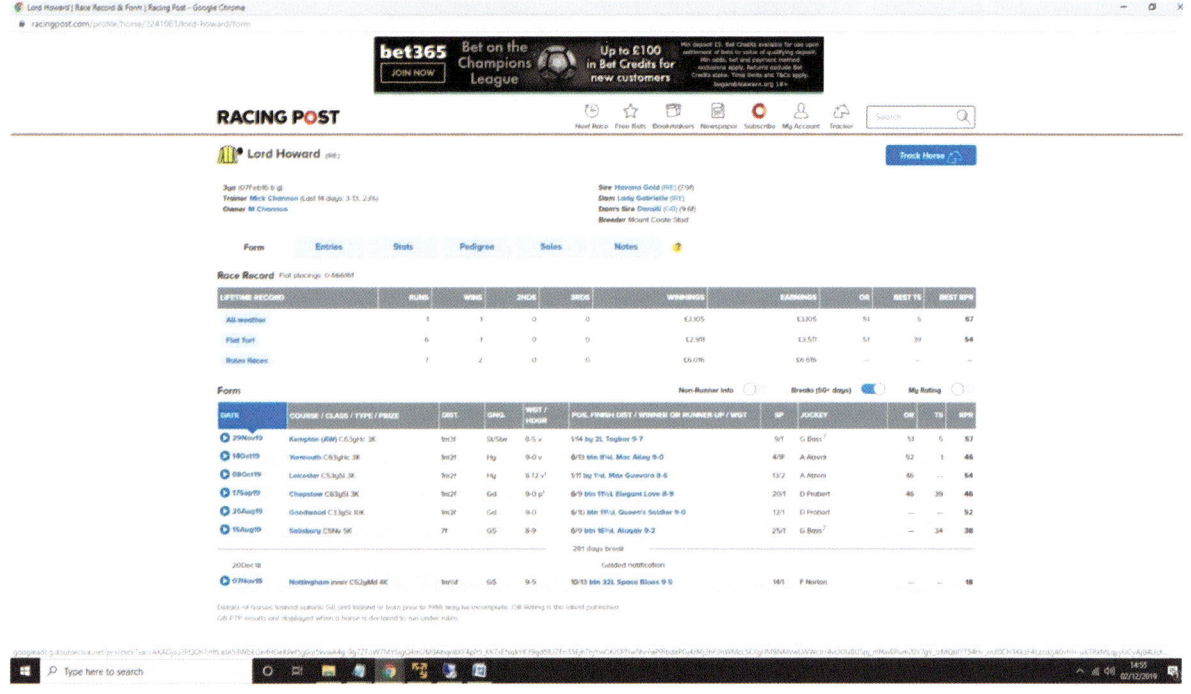

The screenshot above shows total runs as 7 as it includes the race on the 29/11/2019. But at the time of the race the horse had only run 6 times.

You can see from the screenshot the horse Lord Howard last run was on the 8th October 2019 where the horse finished 1st. The horse was carrying weight of 8-12 i.e. 8 stone 12 pounds and had a BHB or Official rating (OR) of 46.

When Lord Howard ran in the race 29th November, 2019 it was carrying weight of 8-5 i.e. 8 stone 5 pounds so the horse was carrying -7 pounds less weight as in it's last qualifying race.

The horse Lord Howard BHB (OR) rating was 46 when it ran on the 8thth October, 2019 as compared to the BHB (OR) to 51 when it ran on the 289th November 2019. So the horse had improved by 5.

Summary

This was a great price. The horse was improving from it's last run from a BHB (OR – Official rating) of 46 to 51 and was carrying -7 pounds less weight as in it's last race back in October 2019.

The horse won the race at a SP of 9/1 but on Betfair the horse traded in-play at 15.0

The horse was gambled on that day as it steamed in from 16/1

Race 7

29th November 2019   Kempton 6.30 Vibrance Winner : 13/8

Class 4

Horse	Result Date	Current BHB	Last BHB	BHB DIFF	WEIGHT DIFF	Last POSITION	Last WIN Date	Total Runs
Jersey Wonder	2019-19-11	86	86	0	2	2	10	10
Pirate King	2019-29-06	82	84	-2	7	3	153	10
Bear Valley	2018-14-04	79	83	-4	17	5	594	25
Dono Di Dio	2019-25-09	78	81	-3	15	4	65	19
Cotton Club	10/02/2019	80	80	0	10	2	58	60
Conkering Hero	2019-19-09	75	73	2	-13	1	71	33
Casa Comigo	2019-19-11	68	68	0	2	3	10	15
Vibrance	**11/05/2019**	**70**	**65**	**5**	**-12**	**1**	**24**	**8**

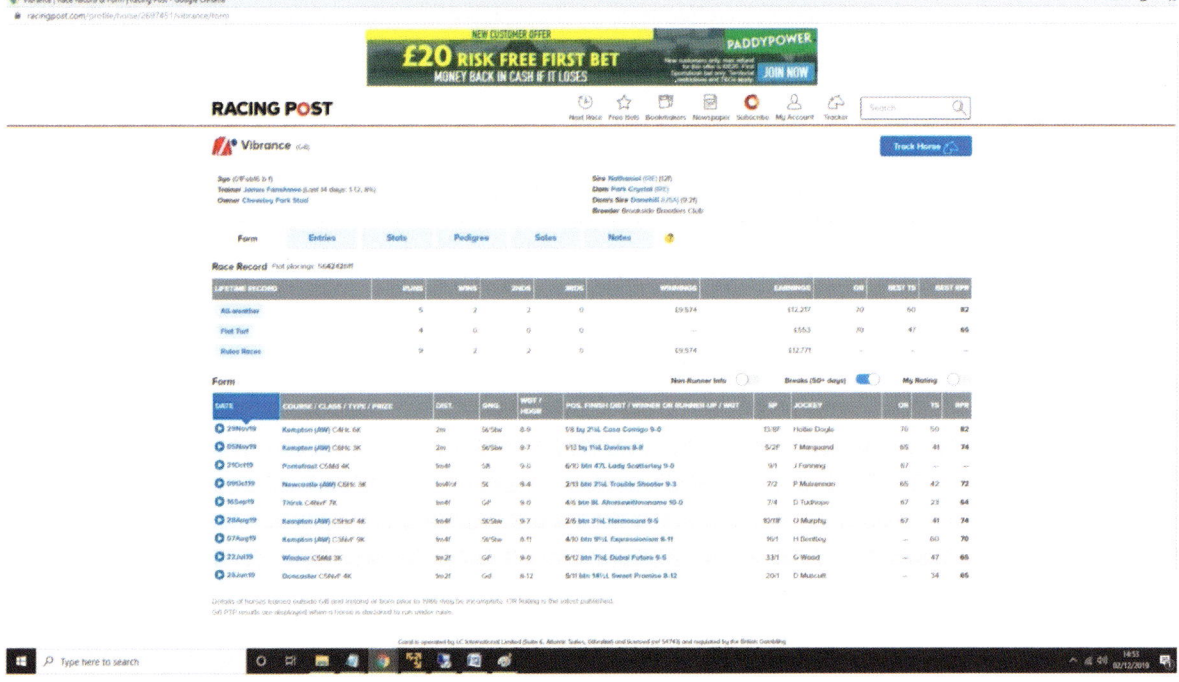

The screenshot above shows total runs as 9 as it includes the race on the 29/11/2019. But at the time of the race the horse had only run 8 times.

You can see from the screenshot the horse Vibrance last run was on the 5th November 2019 where the horse finished 1st. The horse was carrying weight of 9-7 i.e. 9 stone 7 pounds and had a BHB or Official rating (OR) of 65.

When Vibrance ran in the race 29th November, 2019 it was carrying weight of 8-9 i.e. 8 stone 9 pounds so the horse was carrying -12 pounds less weight as in it's last qualifying race.

The horse Vibrance BHB (OR) rating was 65 when it ran on the 05th November, 2019 as compared to the BHB (OR) to 70 when it ran on the 29th November 2019. So the horse had improved by 5.

The horse won the race at a SP of 13/8 but on Betfair the horse traded in-play at 2.52

This is not my type of bet as the price is too low for an handicap.

Race 8 Shows An Example Of A Class 2 race

30th November 2019   Newbury 1.50 Star Of Lanks 3rd : 6/1

Class 2

Horse	Result Date	Current BHB	Last BHB	BHB DIFF	WEIGHT DIFF	Last POSITION	Last WIN Date	Total Runs
Soul Emotion	2018-22-12	150	152	-2	5	5	343	3
Jenkins	2019-25-03	138	145	-7	-4	2	250	18
Lord Napier	04/06/2019	144	144	0	-1	5	238	13
Peter The Mayo Man	2018-20-04	133	142	-9	-9	1	589	19
Limited Reserve	05/11/2019	134	137	-3	10	4	203	16
Coeur Blimey	2019-13-11	131	133	-2	-9	4	17	19
Silver Kayf	11/10/2019	129	130	-1	-15	4	20	15
Howling Milan	2019-27-10	127	130	-3	-18	5	34	5
Star Of Lanka	11/10/2019	**132**	**128**	**4**	**-15**	2	20	**10**
Mr Pumblechook	11/04/2019	125	127	-2	-20	4	26	9
Nordic Combined	2019-13-11	124	124	0	-20	3	17	9
Pride Of Lecale	11/07/2019	122	111	11	-31	1	23	9
The Cashel Man	2019-31-07	130	90	40	25	4	122	4
Downtown Getaway	2019-19-01	131	0	131	-9	1	315	4
Snow Leopardess	2017-27-09	130	0	130	-4	1	794	8

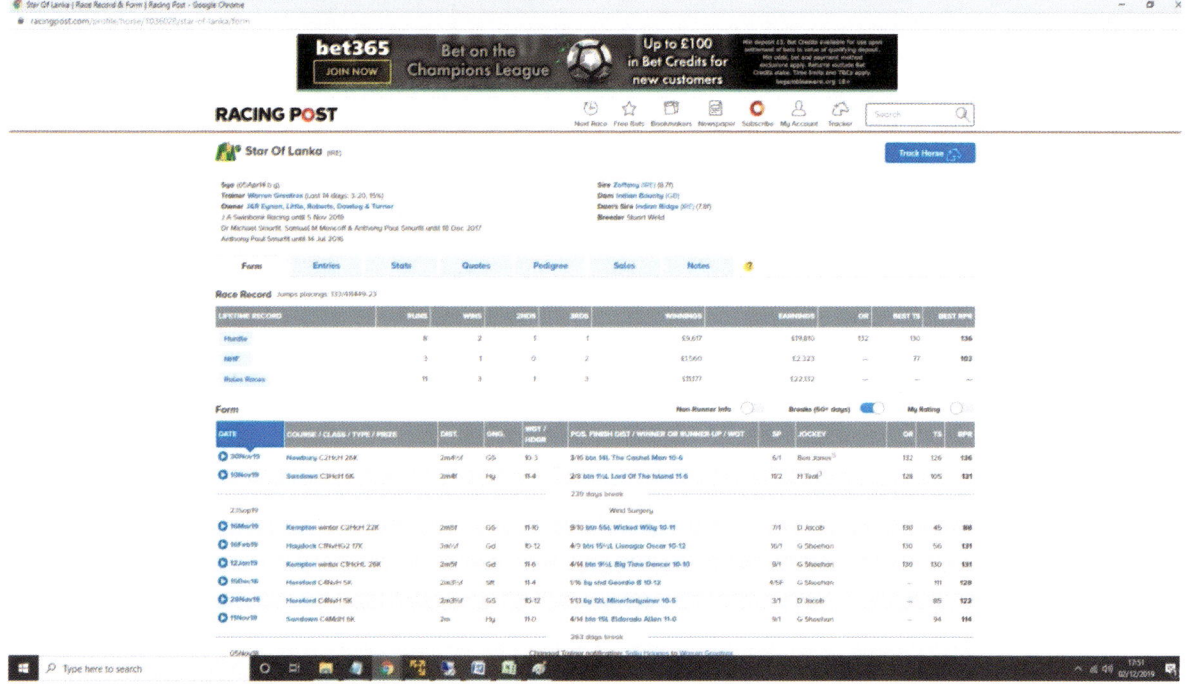

The screenshot above shows total runs as 11 as it includes the race on the 30/11/2019. But at the time of the race the horse had only run 10 times.

You can see from the screenshot the horse Star Of Lanka last run was on the 10th November 2019 where the horse finished 2nd. The horse was carrying weight of 11-4 i.e. 11 stone 4pounds and had a BHB or Official rating (OR) of 128.

When Star Of Lanka ran in the race 30th November, 2019 it was carrying weight of 10-3 i.e. 10 stone 3 pounds so the horse was carrying -15 pounds less weight as in it's last qualifying race.

The horse Star Of Lanka BHB (OR) rating was 128 when it ran on the 10th November, 2019 as compared to the BHB (OR) to 132 when it ran on the 30th November 2019. So the horse had improved by 4.

The horse finished 3rd in the race at a SP of 6/1 but on Betfair the horse traded in-play at minimum odds 4.30 so you could have traded out.

They do not win all the time!

I advise you to ignore races above Class 4and concentrate only Class 4, 5 and Class 6.

Race 9

17th November 2019   Fontwell 12-25 Good News   1st : 11/8F

Class 5

Horse	Result Date	Current BHB	Last BHB	BHB DIFF	WEIGHT DIFF	Last POSITION	Last WIN Date	Total Runs
Pleney	10/04/2019	105	100	5	2	3	44	8
Hold Me Tight	06/05/2019	90	95	-5	-6	3	165	11
Good News	**2019-23-10**	**95**	**90**	**5**	**0**	**1**	**25**	**11**
Polar Light	2019-25-02	87	89	-2	17	2	265	6
Jonnigraig	2019-30-10	83	85	-2	-2	5	18	14
Bluebell Sally	10/09/2019	80	85	-5	5	5	39	5
First Assembly	2019-17-10	91	0	91	9	4	31	5

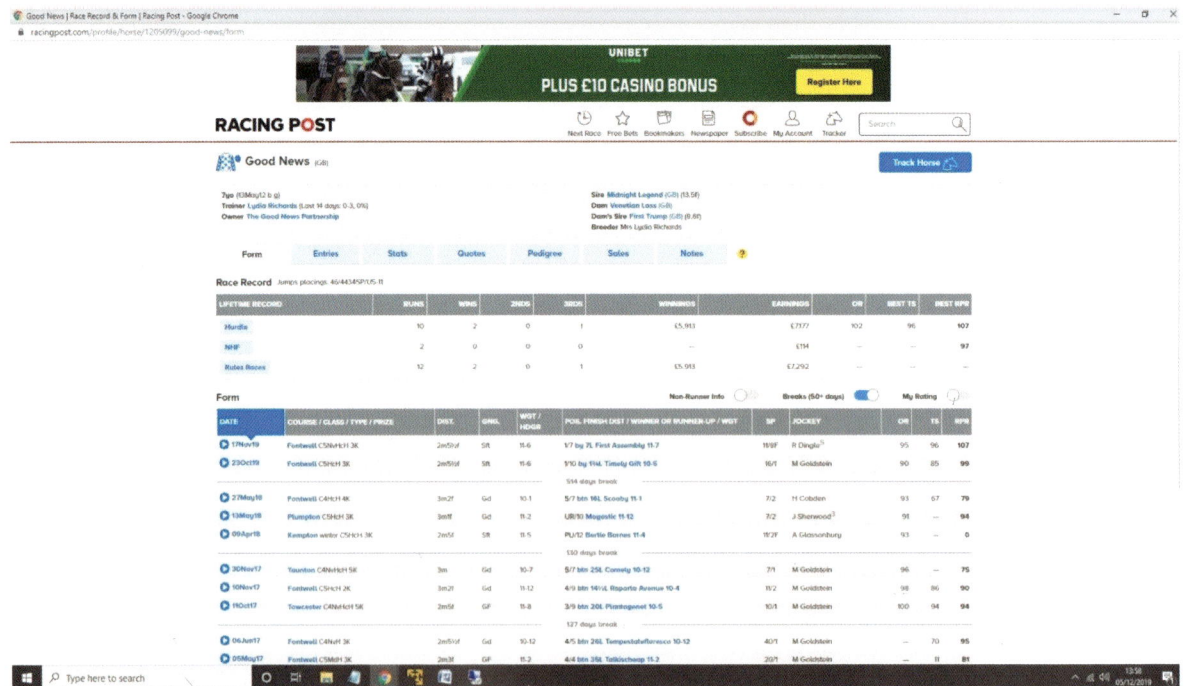

The screenshot above shows total runs as 12 as it includes the race on the 17/11/2019. But at the time of the race the horse had only run 11 times.

You can see from the screenshot the horse Good News last run was on the 23rd October 2019 where the horse finished 1st. The horse was carrying weight of 11-6 i.e. 11 stone 6 pounds and had a BHB or Official rating (OR) of 90.

When Good News ran in the race 17th November, 2019 it was carrying weight of 11-6 i.e. 11 stone 6 pounds so the horse was carrying the same weight as in it's last qualifying race.

The horse Good News a BHB (OR) rating was 90 when it ran on the 23rd October, 2019 as compared to the BHB (OR) to 95 when it ran on the 17th November 2019. So the horse had improved by 5.

The horse finished 1st in the race at a SP of 13/8 but on Betfair the horse traded in-play at maximum odds 7.40.

I always trade at bigger odds on Betfair!

Race 10

5th May 2019   Newmarket 2-55 On The Warpath 1st : 9/4F

Note: Flavius Titus 5/1 was 3rd

Class 2

There were two horses that qualified and I bet on both horses.

Horse	Result Date	Current BHB	Last BHB	BHB DIFF	WEIGHT DIFF	Last POSITION	Last WIN Date	Total Runs
Gifted Master	2018-17-11	109	115	-6	7	5	169	30
On The Warpath	**2019-18-04**	**102**	**101**	**1**	**0**	2	17	**10**
Gunmetal	2018-18-08	104	97	7	5	1	260	21
Summerghand	2019-16-04	100	97	3	-6	2	19	24
Victory Angel	2018-18-08	93	97	-4	-11	3	260	15
Haddaf	10/09/2018	90	96	-6	-11	4	208	20
Giogiobbo	2019-19-04	92	92	0	-10	3	16	7
Flavius Titus	**2019-16-04**	**95**	**91**	**4**	**-5**	1	19	**12**
Hart Stopper	10/03/2018	88	88	0	-11	4	214	20
Lady Dancealot	2018-17-06	87	78	9	-5	5	322	15

I have included two screenshots of both horses **On The Warpath** and **Flavius Titus**.

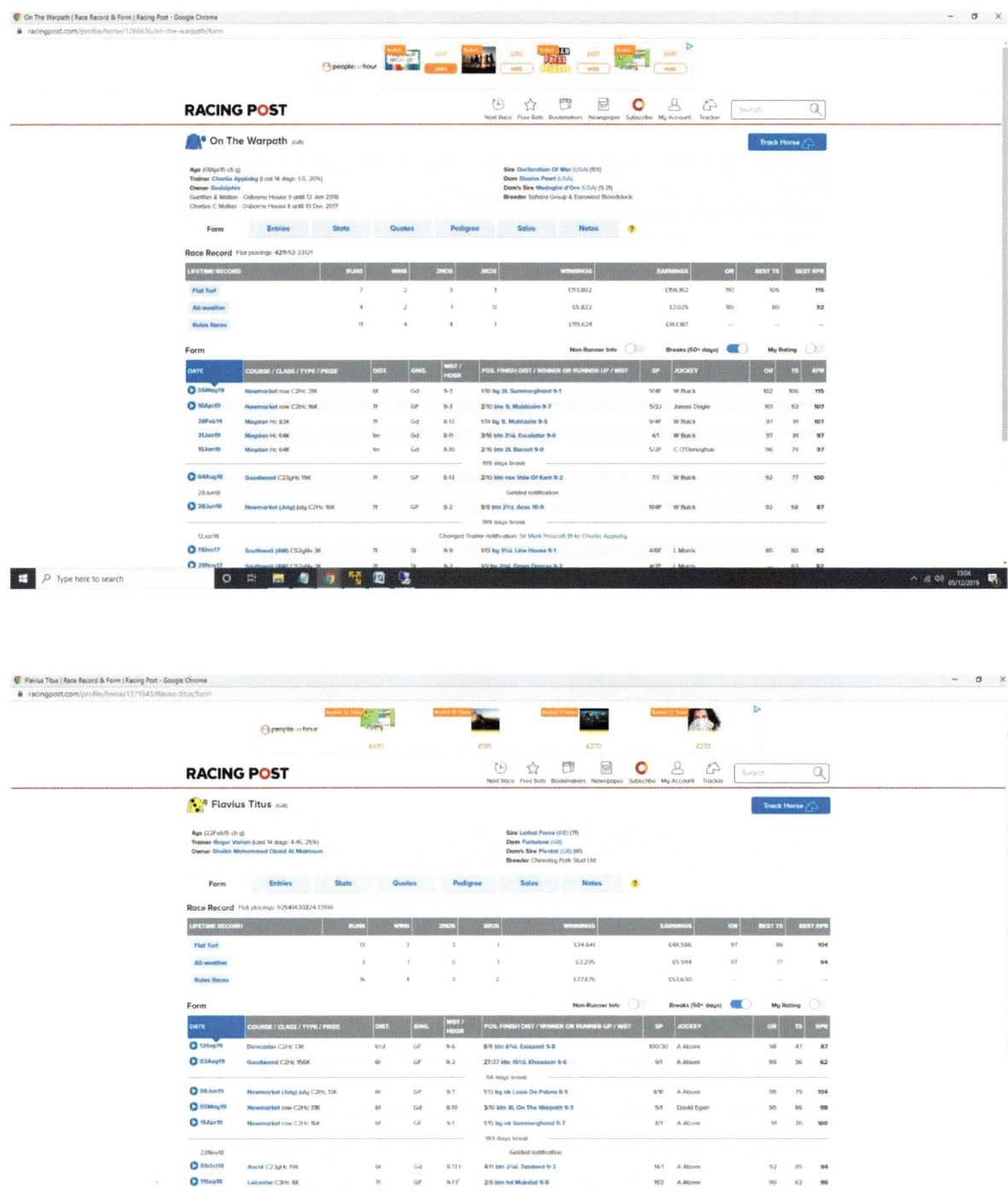

The screenshot above shows total runs as 12 as it includes the race on the 17/11/2019. But at the time of the race the horse had only run 11 times.

I will concentrate on the winning horse here "On The War Path".

You can see from the screenshot the horse On The War Path last run was on the 18th April 2019 where the horse finished 2nd. The horse was carrying weight of 9-3 i.e. 9 stone 3 pounds and had a BHB or Official rating (OR) of 101.

When On The War Path ran in the race 5thth May, 2019 it was carrying weight of 9-3 i.e. 9 stone 3 pounds so the horse was carrying the same weight as in it's last qualifying race.

The horse On The War Path BHB (OR) rating was 101 when it ran on the 18th April, 2019 as compared to the BHB (OR) to 102 when it ran on the 5thth May 2019. So the horse had improved by 1.

The horse finished 1st in the race at a SP of 9/4 but on Betfair the horse traded in-play at maximum odds 12.0.

This is the importance of getting better odds on Betfair In-Play!

Some Other Races

I have showed 10 Races in detail in this eBook but I have listed a few more winners below without the detail so you can practice this UK horse racing handicap system.

4th May 2019 Newmarket 4.10 Moyassar 1st 10/1

Moyassar	2018-31-10	98	94	4	-3	2	185	7

8th May 2019 Chester 3.00 Leodis Dream 1st 9/2 Betfair In-Play 11.0

Leodis Dream	2019-26-04	94	90	4	-1	1	12	5

11th May 2019 Ascot 4.00 Cape Byron 1st 8/1 Betfair In-Play 17.50

Cape Byron	09/08/2018	103	101	2	0	2	245	11

15th May 2019 Bath 7.55 Top Rock Talula 1st 3/1   Betfair In-Play 12.0

| Top Rock Talula | 04/04/2019 | 58 | 57 | 1 | -3 | 2 | 41 | 10 |

27th November 2019 Kempton 7.10 Queen Constantine 1st 8/1 Betfair In-Play 10.50

| Queen Constantine | 08/11/2019 | 75 | 74 | 1 | -12 | 2 | 108 | 11 |

30th July 2019 Yarmouth 4.30 Mitigator 1st 6/1 Betfair In-Play 8.20

| Mitigator | 2019-20-06 | 58 | 55 | 3 | -5 | 1 | 40 | 10 |

30th July 2019 Worcester 8.20 Noah And The Ark 1st 11/4 Betfair In-Play 5.70

| Noah And The Ark | 2019-18-07 | 120 | 115 | 5 | -4 | 1 | 12 | 10 |

5th August 2019 Ripon 5.00 Matewan 1st 9/4F   Betfair In-Play 9.00

| Matewan | 2019-17-06 | 73 | 72 | 1 | -4 | 2 | 49 | 10 |

8th August 2019 Sandown 8.15 Rock The Cradle 1st 5/2F   Betfair In-Play 6.20

| Rock The Cradle | 2019-17-07 | 73 | 70 | 3 | -3 | 2 | 22 | 6 |

10th August 2019 Ascot 2.50 Power Of Darkness 1st 11/4F   Betfair In-Play 5.70

| Power Of Darkness | 2019-26-06 | 94 | 91 | 3 | -3 | 1 | 45 | 7 |

The Betfair Factor

Many punters use standard bookmakers but the better value is in-play betting on these selections on the Betfair exchange as you can see from the race examples in this eBook. When a race is in-play a horse's price will move erratically sometimes spike out to 40.0 or 100.0!

So say a horse is 2/1 (3.0 Betfair) before the race starts you could ask for 10.0 in-play so you can see how much more profit you could make.

Let Me Do The Hard Work!

I produce my handicap ratings daily and if you are interested in receiving these please contact me on Email : agentlease@hotmail.com

I normally email these out before 11am on the day's racing.

I normally charge a small monthly fee of £35 which can be paid to my Paypal account agentlease@hotmail.com

COPYRIGHT 2019 MCHJAP LTD All Rights Reserved.
COPYRIGHT of this publication is strictly reserved.
No part of this publication may be reproduced or transmitted.

Printed in Great Britain
by Amazon